I AM ONE

A BOOK of ACTION

BY SUSAN VERDE · ART BY PETER H. REYNOLDS

Abrams Books for Young Readers · New York

To every ONE.
You make a difference.

– S.V.

To Greta Thunberg, who showed
the world the power of ONE young person.

– P.H.R.

The illustrations in this book were created using ink, gouache, watercolor, and tea.

Cataloging-in-Publication Data has been applied for and
may be obtained from the Library of Congress.

ISBN 978-1-4197-4238-5

Text copyright © 2020 Susan Verde
Illustrations copyright © 2020 Peter H. Reynolds
Reynolds Studio assistance by Julia Anne Young
Book design by Pamela Notarantonio and Jade Rector

Printed and bound in U.S.A.
10 9 8 7 6 5 4 3 2 1

Abrams Books for Young Readers are available at special discounts when purchased in quantity for
premiums and promotions as well as fundraising or educational use. Special editions can also be
created to specification. For details, contact specialsales@abramsbooks.com or the address below.

Abrams® is a registered trademark of Harry N. Abrams, Inc.

ABRAMS The Art of Books
195 Broadway, New York, NY 10007
abramsbooks.com

How do I
make a difference?

It seems like a tall order
for one so small.

But beautiful things
start with just
One.

One seed
to start a garden.

One stroke
to start a masterpiece.

One note
to start a melody.

One step
to start a journey.

One brick
to start breaking down walls.

And I can speak
One gentle word
to start a conversation.

I can use my
One soft voice
to start a friendship.

I can perform
One act of kindness
to start a connection.

I can share
One tender hug
to start caring.

I can light One candle
to start leading the way.

I can make
One drop in the water...

to start ripples...

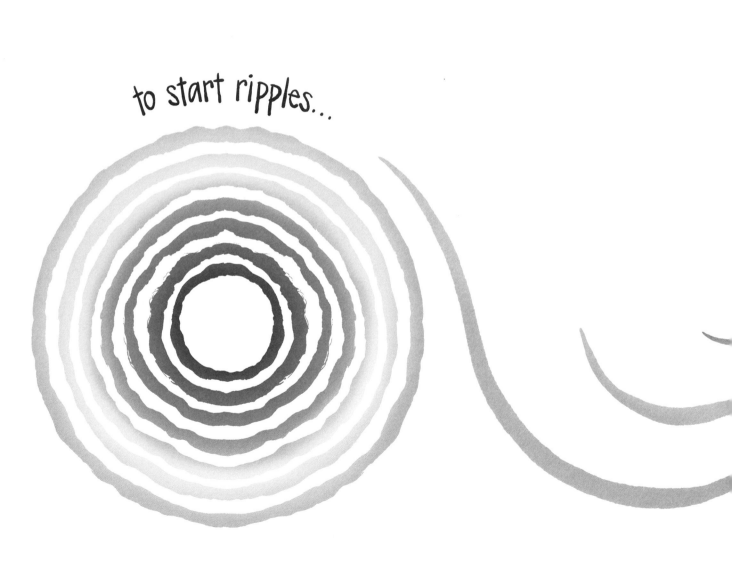

that become swells, then waves,

traveling over oceans...

across borders
and boundaries...

landing on distant shores

to start a chain reaction,
inspire a movement,
make a change.

I am One.
And I can take action.

We are each One.
And we can take action.

One by One,
we can make a difference.

Because ONE is all it takes...

to start something beautiful.

Author's Note

Sometimes it can feel like there are so many issues facing the world these days that we wonder how, as one individual, we can make a difference. *I Am One* was inspired by a quote from the Dalai Lama: "Just as ripples spread out when a single pebble is dropped into water, the actions of individuals can have far-reaching effects."

Indeed, incredible things can begin with just One. Just as a beautiful garden starts with one seed, all of the marches and collective movements we witness and participate in started with one idea, one step, one voice, one act of kindness—and we can take our own first step to make the world a better, more united, and more peaceful place. We are all activists.

So how do we begin? Following is a mindfulness meditation and a self-reflection activity to help you get started.

Mindfulness is about being in the present moment and paying attention to your life here and now. When we feel strongly about something and want to make a change or take action against something we feel isn't okay in our world, we need to be present and access the problem-solving, creative, compassionate parts of our brains. It is alright to feel passionate or even angry, but real change doesn't come when we are lost in our emotions and reacting; it comes when we decide intentionally—and with an open heart and clear mind—how we want to respond. The following meditation can help you get into that mindset; it is also a wonderful way to take care of yourself while you are doing the work to make a difference.

- Find a comfortable seat. Close your eyes. Place your hands on your belly, and breathe slowly in and out through your nose. Notice your breath and your belly moving in and out.
- Now think about something you would like to help with or a change you want to see—in the world, in your neighborhood, in your school, or wherever it is. Notice any feelings that come up. Maybe you are angry or sad or frustrated. Don't try to stop those feelings; instead, name them in your mind.
- Now bring your attention back to your breath. Try to find a slow rhythm, breathing in and out, and imagine each breath filling your whole body. As you breathe in, say to yourself, "I am strong." As you breathe out, say, "I am focused."
- Repeat this a few more times. Slowly open your eyes. Notice how you feel.

At the end of this meditation, write down or tell someone what came to your mind.
Ask yourself:
- What did you think about that needs changing?
- What feelings did you have when you thought about it?
- What can you do, now that you are focused and strong—what first step can you take—to be the one to make a difference?

You are ready! Remember, no act is too small. You can be that pebble causing ripples that reach far and wide. You are ONE, and that is how it starts.

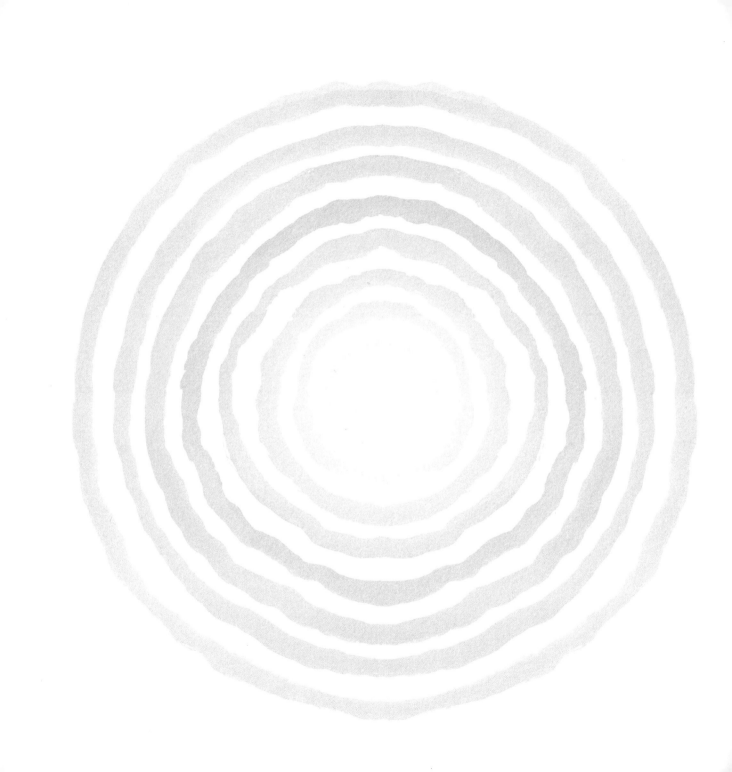

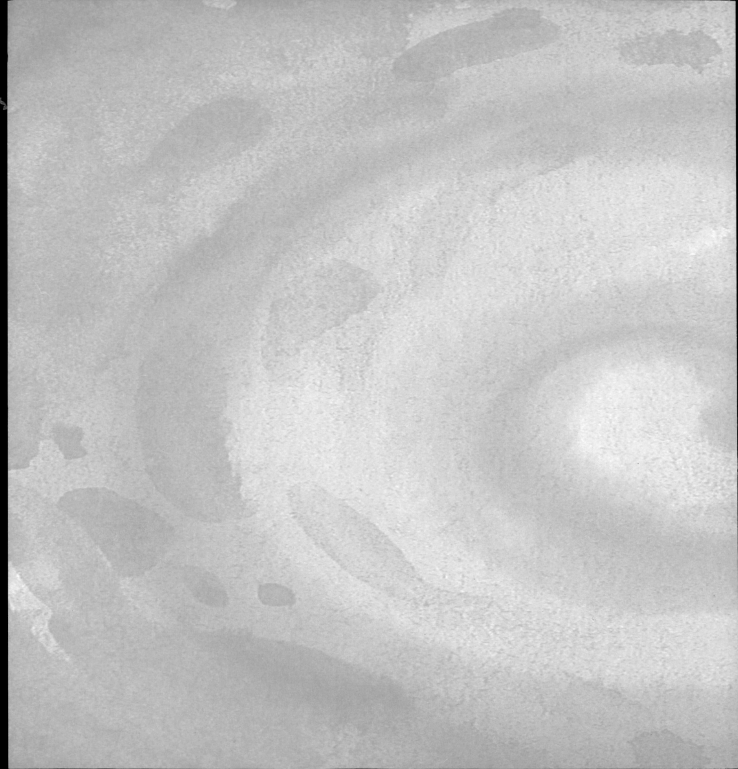